Pebble®
Bilingüe/
Bilingual

Algunos niños son sordos /
Some Kids Are Deaf

por/by Lola M. Schaefer

Editor Consultor/Consulting Editor: Dra. Gail Saunders-Smith
Consultor/Consultant: Judith M. Gilliam
Former Board Member, National Association for the Deaf

CAPSTONE PRESS
a capstone imprint

Pebble Books are published by Capstone Press,
151 Good Counsel Drive, P.O. Box 669, Mankato, Minnesota 56002.
www.capstonepress.com

092009
005618CGS10

Library of Congress Cataloging-in-Publication Data
Schaefer, Lola M., 1950–
      [Some kids are deaf. Spanish]
      Algunos niños son sordos / por Lola M. Schaefer = Some kids are deaf /
by Lola M. Schaefer.
      p. cm. — (Understanding differences = Comprendiendo las diferencias)
      Includes index.
      Summary: "Simple text and photographs describe kids who are deaf, the ways
they communicate, and some of their everyday activities — in both English and
Spanish" — Provided by publisher.
      ISBN 978-1-4296-4591-1 (library binding)
      1. Deaf children — Juvenile literature. 2. Deafness — Juvenile literature. I. Title.
II. Title: Some kids are deaf. III. Series.
HV2392.S3318 2010
362.4′2 — dc22   2009030376

Note to Parents and Teachers

The Comprendiendo las diferencias/Understanding Differences set supports national
social studies standards related to individual development and identity. This book
describes children who are deaf and illustrates their special needs in both English
and Spanish. The photographs support early readers in understanding the text. The
repetition of words and phrases helps early readers learn new words. This book also
introduces early readers to subject-specific vocabulary words, which are defined in the
Glossary. Early readers may need assistance to read some words and to use the Table of
Contents, Glossary, Internet Sites, and Index sections of the book.

Table of Contents

Tabla de contenidos

Deafness

Some kids are deaf.
Kids who are deaf
cannot hear.

La sordera

Algunos niños son sordos.
Los niños que son sordos
no pueden oír.

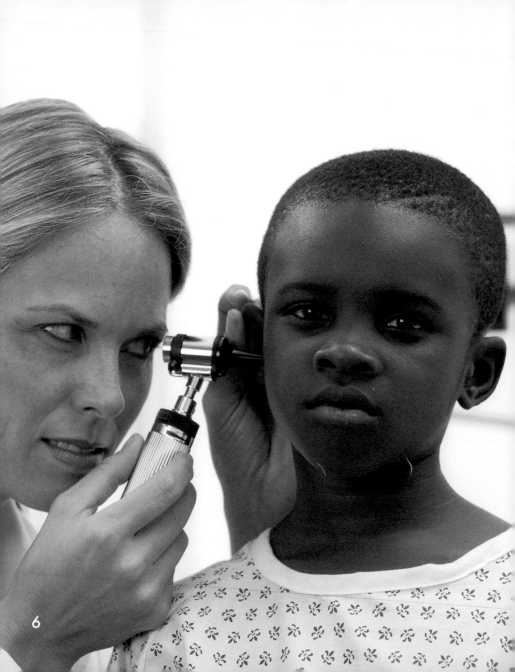

Some kids are born deaf.
Other kids become deaf
from a sickness or from
getting hurt.

Algunos niños son sordos
cuando nacen. Algunos niños
quedan sordos por una
enfermedad o una lesión.

8

Tools for Hearing

Some kids can hear a little.
They wear hearing aids
to hear sounds louder.

Herramientas para oír

Algunos niños pueden oír algo.
Ellos usan audífonos para oír
sonidos más fuertemente.

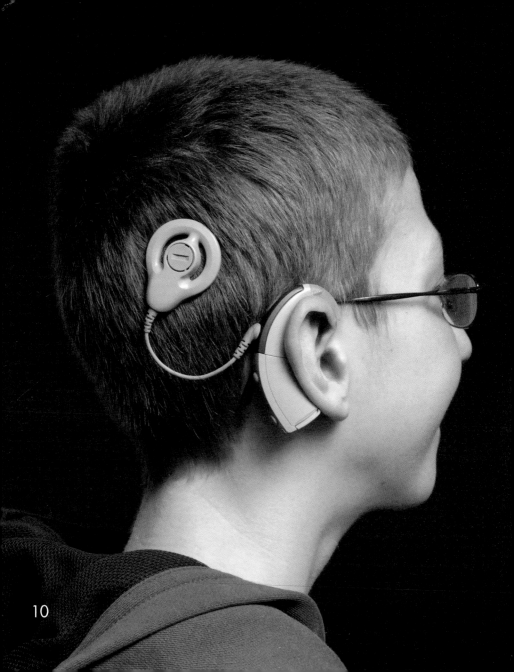

Some kids who are deaf get cochlear implants. Implants help them hear some sounds.

Algunos niños sordos reciben implantes cocleares. Los implantes los ayudan a oír algunos sonidos.

BRAIN TEASER!

Sign Language / Lenguaje de señas

1

2

You are/Tú eres   my/mi   friend/amigo

12

Talking

Some kids who are deaf
use sign language to talk.
Sign language is hand signs
that stand for letters, words,
and numbers.

Hablar

Algunos niños sordos usan el
lenguaje de señas para hablar.
El lenguaje de señas es una
serie de señas hechas con
las manos que representan
letras, palabras y números.

13

Some kids who are deaf
use their voice to talk.
Speech therapists teach
them to speak clearly.

Algunos niños sordos
usan su voz para hablar.
Los terapistas del habla les
enseñan a hablar claramente.

Everyday Life

Kids who are deaf depend on their sense of sight. Flashing lights tell them it's time for class.

La vida diaria

Los niños sordos dependen de su sentido de la vista. Luces intermitentes anuncian cuando es hora de ir a la clase.

STRADDLING THE EQUATOR,
MACAPA, BRAZIL IS AN EXOTIC WORLD

18

Kids who are deaf watch
TV with closed captioning.
The words tell what people
on TV are saying.

Los niños sordos miran
televisión con subtítulos.
Las palabras muestran lo
que dicen las personas
en televisión.

20

Kids who are deaf depend
on their sense of touch.
They can feel a pager
vibrate when a friend
sends a text message.

Los niños sordos dependen
de su sentido del tacto.
Ellos pueden sentir la vibración
de un buscapersonas de texto
cuando un amigo les envía
un mensaje de texto.

Glossary

cochlear implant — a small electronic device that is surgically put into a person's head; cochlear implants allow sounds to get to the brain.

hearing aid — a small electronic device that people wear in or behind one or both ears

pager — a small electronic device that can receive and send text messages

senses — ways of learning about your surroundings; hearing, smelling, touching, tasting, and sight are the five senses.

speech therapist — a person who is trained to help people learn to speak clearly

text message — words sent from a pager or cell phone to another person's pager or cell phone

FactHound offers a safe, fun way to find Internet sites related to this book. All of the sites on FactHound have been researched by our staff.

Here's how:

Visit *www.facthound.com*

FactHound will fetch the best sites for you!

Glosario

el audífono — un dispositivo electrónico pequeño que las personas usan dentro o detrás de uno o de los dos oídos

el buscapersonas de texto — un dispositivo electrónico pequeño que puede enviar y recibir mensajes de texto

el implante coclear — un pequeño dispositivo electrónico que es colocado quirúrgicamente en la cabeza de una persona; los implantes cocleares permiten que los sonidos lleguen al cerebro.

el mensaje de texto — palabras enviadas de un buscapersonas o teléfono celular al buscapersonas o teléfono celular de otra persona

los sentidos — maneras de aprender acerca de tus alrededores; los cinco sentidos son el oído, el olfato, el tacto, el gusto y la vista.

el terapista del habla — una persona capacitada para ayudar a personas a hablar claramente

Sitios de Internet

FactHound brinda una forma segura y divertida de encontrar sitios de Internet relacionados con este libro. Todos los sitios en FactHound han sido investigados por nuestro personal.

Esto es todo lo que tú necesitas hacer:

Visita *www.facthound.com*

¡FactHound buscará los mejores sitios para ti!

Index

Índice

Editorial Credits

Strictly Spanish, translation services; Katy Kudela, bilingual editor; Bob Lentz, designer; Eric Mankse, production specialist

Photo Credits

Arthur Tilley/FPG International LLC, 6
Capstone Press/Karon Dubke, cover, 4, 8, 10, 12, 14, 16, 18, 20